Tent Revival

Jo Hammers

Paranormal Crossroads & Publishing

Tent Revival

ISBN 978-0-9911540-5-0

www.paranormalcrossroads.com

This work is fiction. All of the characters, organizations, and events portrayed in this novel are either products of the author's imagination or are used fictitiously.

Cover Art by Jo Hammers, 2017.

Table of Contents

Tent Revival

Jo Hammers

Paranormal Crossroads & Publishing

INTRODUCTION

Most male ministers believe that women cannot be preachers; that their place is at home, barefoot, and pregnant; being a door mat for their husbands. They say a woman preaching would be usurping her authority over the man whom God has made the head of her. Men demean and put women down in order to make them-selves look bigger. A minister, who verbally assaults a woman called to preach, is probably a wife abuser as well. Those who assault women verbally are dark beings, not light beings.

I am a writer, but I am also called to build ten churches. My building will be thru my written words calling women to preach and to become church pastors. When ten answer their call and build their first 'Three Chair Church', I have fulfilled my mission/my unusual calling.

I am the trumpet sound calling women to the ministry and the building of new Pentecostal, Holy Ghost filled churches that will be part of the New Age that is coming in. The New Testament age replaced the Old Testament Age. Now a New Age/ Third Testament era of Holy Ghost power is about to fall like rain. Some refer to the end time rain falling as the 'Latter Rain'.

There are many 'John the Baptist' types that will be the fore-runners of God's last day and Third Testament Age of Holy Ghost power rain/spirit being poured out upon the Earth. I am a 'John the Baptist' type, a trumpet sound calling women to the new day and to the ministry.

CHAPTER ONE

The Pentecostal Tent Show

It was springtime in Sandy Soil, Texas. School was just a few weeks from being out for the summer, and the youth in the one horse town of 176 inhabitants were bored. There was no movie house, fast food restaurants, or other forms of entertainment. There wasn't even a gas station. The only social outlets in the town were one tiny mom and pop grocery market, and two small churches. One of the churches was Catholic and the other was God Assembly Protestant.

It came as a welcome surprise, to relieve boredom, when a Pentecostal lady evangelist set up a tent next to the mom and pop market to hold a revival. All the children and teens of the tiny town saw the tent meeting as a chance to go down, sit on the back rows of folding chairs, and socialize for the evening with their friends, while they watched the odd things that Pentecostals did in their services; like speaking in tongues and dancing in the spirit. To the children, it was like getting to go to a movie and sit on the back row. The folding chairs on the back row of the tent revival were coveted by the youth of the small town, because no parents could sit behind them to monitor whatever they did.

Carlotta Garcia, like the other kids in the small town, begged her Catholic mother (Rosa) to let her go down and watch the event with her friends. Rosa Garcia, Carlotta's mother agreed, not wanting her daughter to miss out on any social events with her friends. She had dreams of her Carlotta one day being high school prom queen, even though she was now only thirteen. A girl had to be social with other kids, if she wanted their votes when it came time for them to vote for prom night royalty. Rosa Garcia had long term goals set in her head for her daughter. So, Rosa let thirteen year old Carlotta and Pablo, her eleven year old son, go down to the tent meeting to socialize and watch the Pentecostal's tent show. Rosa felt that letting her children go watch the Pentecostals show couldn't be any worse than letting them watch the monster movies her husband Hidalgo rented on weekends for entertainment. Rosa felt sure the Pentecostal's floor show would just be a different type of monster movie evening.

Given permission, Carlotta and Pablo went early to claim folding chair seats on the back row. There were 11 other children in the small town that were old enough to attend without a parent accompanying them. They met Carlotta and Pablo there, and they also claimed their back row seats and settled in laughing and socializing till the Pentecostal revival show started. The youngest child was nine, and the oldest was seventeen. Carlotta was thirteen, and her brother Pablo was eleven.

In front of the children, seated in a folding chair a couple rows forward, was a local woman known as Edith White Suit. Edith was a local character. She always dressed in white; in high necks, long sleeves, and long skirts, no matter how hot it was. Also, she never wore shoes. She always walked barefoot wherever she went. The first night of the Pentecostal's tent meeting was no different. She sat in front of the children barefoot and dressed in white. A very slight breeze was blowing. Wisps of Edith's red hair floated on the gentle wind that seemed only to blow on her.

However, her hair did not look out of place or windblown.

Pablo elbowed his sister and whispered, "Look . . . Edith White Suit has a huge bee that has landed in the top of her hair. One of its wings seems to be snagged in her curls. Be ready to laugh when it stings her. I bet she jumps out of that White Suit she is wearing."

Carlotta turned from chatting with her friends and eyed the top of Edith White Suit's head. Sure enough, a bee had landed in the top of her curly hair and was in a frenzy trying to free its wing. Edith White Suit was indeed about to be stung. Carlotta jumped to her feet and clumsily parted the two rows of folding chairs in front of her, to make her way to the White Suited woman to swat the bee from her hair. Carlotta was a person of compassion.

Reaching the back of Edith White Suit's folding chair, thirteen year old Carlotta quickly raised her right hand, aimed, and swatted the bee from Edith's curly hair. The mad bee went tumbling thru the air and then landed in the aisle's sandy soil. After a brief moment of regaining its composure, the bee flew away to be seen no more.

Startled, Edith White Suit turned around quickly to see who had been messing with her hair.

"I am sorry, Edith White Suit. You had a bee in your hair. I just knocked it out to keep you from getting stung." Carlotta quickly explained.

"You have come to my defense. Thank you, Carlotta. I now owe you one. Should you need to be rescued from a devil bee or a devil in human flesh, I will come to your aid. Just yell, 'Edith White Suit.'"

Carlotta snickered and then said, "Thank you for not being mad at me for swatting your hair, Edith White Suit. My mother would kill me if she ever found out I messed with you. She says you are a gringo Protestant."

"I am not Catholic, or Protestant . . . Carlotta." I am . . . a friend of God, you might say." Edith White Suit replied smiling. "Now I am a friend of you."

"Friends we will be!" Carlotta replied and then added, "I have a friend named Wendy at school. She is not Catholic. She calls herself a Baptist. I don't mind that she is Baptist. Do you mind that I am Catholic, Edith White Suit?" Carlotta asked.

"We all start our spiritual journeys somewhere." Edith replied. "Once upon a time, I was a member of the God Assembly. You don't mind if I am holiness Pentecostal?" Edith asked, smiling sweetly.

"No, I do not mind, Edith White Suit."

"Tonight you will make a new choice Carlotta and you will be Catholic no longer. A big change of spiritual paths is coming to you."

"I won't be Catholic anymore?" replied Carlotta in a confused, questioning voice.

"No, you will not. You are the reason I am here tonight." Edith White Suit stated. God plans to meet you tonight."

"Me . . . God is going to come down and meet me here . . . tonight?"

"Tonight is a special night Carlotta. It is the night of your calling."

"Calling to what?" Carlotta asked again in confusion.

"Just wait and see Carlotta. Pay attention to the service. You will know when you hear your calling and what it is for. You will walk away from this tent meeting tonight with a gift from God. It will be Holy Ghost power. I am here to witness it."

"A gift from God is welcome, Edith White Suit. Do you think I will get to choose the gift he gives me? If I have a choice, I would like God to teach me to toe dance like my friend Wendy at school. She stands on her toes and ballet dances. To me, that would be the greatest gift ever."

"Toe dancing it is, Carlotta." Edith White Suit stated all smiles. "Tonight you shall dance in the Spirit of God. Holy Ghost dancing is a far better dancing gift than the twinkle toe ballet your friend does."

With that said, Carlotta returned to the back row of folding chairs to socialize with her friends till service started, not giving her conversation with Edith White Suit any further consideration. However, before the service ended, Carlotta answered an altar call given by the lady evangelist. The Pentecostal holiness lady preacher promised that everyone who would come down to her altar would be filled with the Pentecostal's Holy Ghost; and that they would speak in tongues and dance in the spirit of God. Carlotta Garcia was first to go down. She wanted her gift of dancing. The lady evangelist prayed once, touching Carlotta on the forehead. Carlotta was filled with the Pentecostal's Holy Ghost. She then spoke in tongues and danced in the Spirit of God, just like Edith White Suit had promised.

While dancing in the Holy Ghost, Carlotta had a vision in which Jesus spoke to her and called her to preach the gospel. Standing beside Jesus in the vision was a barefoot, smiling Edith White Suit.

CHAPTER TWO

Picking Up a Serpent

"Mama . . . !" screamed Pablo Garcia as he burst thru the front screen door of his parents little two bedroom casa in Sandy Soil, Texas. In his hand, held out from his body, was the wiggling, slithering, coiling body of an extremely angry Rattlesnake. From the look on his frightened face, his mother, Rosa, could see that he was about to collapse in hysteria. Beads of perspiration were running down his cheeks.

"Oh my god, don't move!" shouted Rosa, his short plump Hispanic mother. She instantly dropped the dough that she was forming into little balls in preparation to make tortillas. Immediately, she made the sign of the cross as perspiration instantly popped out on her own forehead. "Don't move, and don't let go of the snake, Pedro. If you let go, it will strike you."

"I am not moving, mama!" he replied in a breaking voice.

Rosa Garcia moved slowly toward her kitchen sink area to retrieve a butcher knife that was resting there on the cabinet top. She knew it would be up to her to rescue her son from the hand held Rattle snake.

Half deaf and not knowing that anything was happening in the kitchen, grandmother (Benita Garcia) entered from an enclosed back porch room that was used as a bedroom by her.

Seeing the snake, the elderly 80 year old Benita grabbed the area of her heart and gasped. She then moved backwards flattening herself against the door frame to her room.

"A . . . a . . . snake. . . . What is Pablo doing with that fang showing, open mouthed, mad snake? She inquired in a raised, distressed, broken voice.

"Be quiet!" Mama Rosa stated sternly, half whispering, as she continued to move toward the cabinet where her butcher knife laid.

About that time, Hidalgo Garcia walked into the kitchen carrying a dead Jack Rabbit by its hind legs. He had hunted the rabbit in the desert back of their house, so they would have meat, for the next meal. Seeing the live Rattlesnake wiggling in the hand of his one and only son, he quickly assessed the life and death situation his eleven year old son was in. It would be up to him to kill the snake, before the snake killed his Pablo. His heart jumped into his throat.

"Don't move, Pablo. Don't lower your arm." Hidalgo quickly informed his son. With that said, Hidalgo Garcia pulled a small hunting knife from the leather sheath attached to the belt in his jeans. Approaching the boy from behind, with a quick flick of his wrist, he cut the snakes body off with one quick slice with his knife, leaving the head still in his son's hand. Then he said, "When I count to three, throw the head quickly, son. It is still alive and able to strike one more time before it dies. Throw it fast and away from you on the count of three. Do you understand?"

"Yes, papa, throw the snake on the count of three." Pablo repeated in a frightened, shaky voice.

"One . . . two . . . three!" counted Hidalgo Garcia in a controlled, but stressed voice.

Instantly, the excited sweating boy threw the snake head in a frenzy, only to throw it in the wrong direction. It went flying with fangs showing toward the elderly grandmother, who immediately fainted. The opened mouthed snake head flew within inches of her ear. Them, it flew thru the open doorway by her and landed on her enclosed porch, bedroom's floor.

Rosa Garcia immediately screamed and ran to the grandmother's fainted body to see if she had been bitten. After a moment of slapping the grandmother's cheeks, Benita Garcia opened her elderly eyes and then scrambled to sit up quickly in a panic, thinking she had possibly been bitten.

"The snake . . . the snake where is it? Where did it bite me?" Grandmother Benita demanded in a frightened voice.

"The Rattle snake is dead in your bedroom floor, Benita." Rosa stated quickly, while making a quick sign of the cross. "You are safe."

After calming herself for a moment or so, Rosa became instantly in an outrage with her son. She rose from the side of the grandmother and grabbed Pablo by the neck of his shirt and screamed, "What do you mean bringing a live snake in this house. One of us could have died from your stupidity."

"It is Carlotta's fault . . . ," he sputtered.

Rosa then started whopping Pablo's backside with one of her fat hands. Mama Rosa was a fluffy woman. In other words, she was rather on the fat side. She could deliver a mean wallop.

16

"It is not my fault mama."Pablo yelled as his mother beat his back side. Carlotta caused me to catch the snake. Don't blame me. Her Holy Ghost made me do it."

"What?" Rosa demanded, as she quit beating her son's backside.

"Carlotta was out there in your flower bed twirling and dancing under the influence of her Holy Ghost devil, you know the one that she brought home from the Protestant's tent meeting. I walked up to watch her dance. When I did, I spotted the Rattle Snake about to strike her toe dancing foot. I sneaked up behind the snake and caught it by the neck, just before it struck her. After I had it by the neck, I was unable to let it go because it was mad and had its mouth open ready to strike. It is Carlotta's fault."

"You saved her from the snake?" Rosa asked, while eyeing the boy's eyes to see if she thought he was telling her the truth.

"She was lost in that Holy Ghost devil dancing she does. I yelled snake over and over, but she did not hear me. I had to pick up the Rattlesnake to save her."

"Are you telling me that she was out there doing that gringo Holy Ghost Toe Tapping, Protestant dance thing again, and in my flower garden?" Mama Garcia sputtered, asking in disgust.

"Yes, mama, Carlotta and her Holy Ghost spirit have been dancing again, and in your flower bed. You had better call the priest mama. "I think she needs an exorcism," he stated big eyed, and in a serious voice.

"I don't need a priest to do an exorcism." Rosa screeched in anger. "I am going to beat that Holy Ghost spirit out of her with my broom for trampling and dancing in my flowers, not to mention putting you at risk with a Rattle Snake."

CHAPTER THREE

Broom Chase

E xtremely angry and losing her cool, Rosa grabbed her broom and headed outside to give her thirteen year old, Holy Ghost possessed daughter a much needed reality check. Walking briskly, she made her way to her flower bed that her Catholic priest had sprinkled holy water on so flowers would grow. Carlotta was there, just as Pablo had said, standing in her flowers. Raising her broom, she began to screech and scream at her daughter.

Carlotta, having just returned to reality from one of her Holy Ghost toe tapping dancing episodes, ran seeing that her mama Rosa was about to take a broom to her. The faster she ran, the faster her mama Rosa ran. Carlotta ran out her front yard gate onto the sandy soil dirt road in front of their little adobe casa. Her mother was hot on her heels, swinging her broom wildly at Carlotta's backside. Down the sandy soil road they ran toward the Catholic Church, a couple or so blocks down.

"It was not me, mama! It was God and the Holy Ghost that danced in your flower bed." Carlotta shouted as she run down the sandy soil dirt road, occasionally turning to look over her shoulder to see if her mother was about to overtake her.

Rosa was indeed chasing Carlotta with no intentions of giving up. She was one mad little Hispanic woman. Anger oozed from her like perspiration. Reaching the steps of the Catholic Church, Carlotta sprinted up the steps, opened the massive door, and took refuge inside the foyer. She decided she would hide in the confessional if she had to.

Rosa Garcia stopped just in front of her Catholic church's entry door panting. She lowered her broom and tried to regain her composure. There was no way she could enter her holy church swinging a broom at her child. Taking a deep breath, she calmed herself and turned to walk back home in disgust, and to finish her morning chores. At least, Carlotta was in church. Perhaps she would go to confession while in there and her Holy Ghost demon would take a hike.

Walking back towards her home in a huff, Rosa encountered Edith White Suit on the road walking barefoot towards her.

"Lovely day, isn't it?" Edit white Suit greeted as she pointed to the blue of the sky.

Rosa stopped, and rested her broom's straws down on the sandy dirt road. It would be impolite for her not to return a quick greeting and chat for a moment with the odd gringo woman who always wore a long sleeved white suit, no matter how hot it was. No one seemed to know where Edith White Suit lived. When seen, she was always encountered on the town's road between the Catholic Church and the God Assembly church which were about the equivalent of five or so blocks apart on the same road.

Edith White Suit was definitely not Catholic. Rosa attended her Catholic church regularly and Edith White Suit definitely was not a member. The Catholics who lived on the sandy road believed that Edith White Suit was some sort of sister, a nun type in the God Assembly church and possibly lived in the back of it, like the two catholic nuns lived in a little apartment behind the Catholic Church.

"It is not a good day for me, Edith White Suit. My daughter went down to that Pentecostal holiness lady's tent meeting in the field next to the market. She came home the first night possessed by a spirit she calls the Holy Ghost. The Ghost devil makes her dance in my flower garden. I am just beside myself dealing with her. I am sure that I am going to have to ask my priest for an exorcism for her. She quivers, shakes, speaks in a language I don't understand, spins in circles, and dances. That Pentecostal woman tent evangelist put a curse on my Carlotta."

Edith White Suit bit her lip to keep a snicker from escaping. "Tell me about it!" she managed to say without laughing.

"I fear my daughter will be excommunicated from my church, if I don't get her freed from this Holy Ghost spirit that is making her do maddening things. She says she is called to be a gringo, Protestant, Pentecostal, woman minister. She is demon possessed and slipping into insanity, Edith White Head. Women cannot be. The tent woman cursed her."

"Carlotta is not cursed or crazy, Rosa. She has a calling on her life. The Holy Ghost speaking thru her is the voice that carries messages down to us from God."

"You are wrong, Edith White Suit. My Carlotta has become a gringo, possessed, Pentecostal witch."

"Carlotta is not a witch. Rosa. She is a vessel of God, a called one, a chosen one."

"Well, Edith White Suit. You are wrong. Carlotta is possessed and I intend to get that Holy Ghost devil out of her, even if I have to beat him out of her with my broom. I am Catholic. Carlotta is Catholic. Anyone not Catholic is not a member of God's one and only true church." Rosa stated as she turned and walked away in a huff.

Rosa returned home mumbling and sputtering in righteous indignation. She would show, Edith White suit. She would have Father Juan perform an exorcism, just as soon as she could get up enough courage to go to confessional and admit that she had let her daughter attend the gringo Pentecostal lady minister's tent revival.

Back in her kitchen, Rosa was relieved to find that her husband, Hidalgo, had removed the dead snake head and its body from the house while she was gone. Grandmother Benita, on her knees with a scrub brush, apparently had cleaned up the snake's blood.

CHAPTER FOUR

Father Juan's Fall

Peeping out the massive wood door of her family's Catholic Church, Carlotta watched as her mother angrily walked away back down the sandy dirt road toward their home. Suddenly, Carlotta was surprised to hear the voice of Father Juan speaking to her from behind her.

"Are you taking refuge in the church this morning for some reason, Carlotta?" Father Juan asked as she spun about to face him in his long black robe.

"My mother was chasing me with her broom. I . . . er . . . uh . . . was in her flower bed. You know how annoyed she gets when anyone steps onto the holy ground beneath her flowers."

"Would you like to tell me about it in the confessional?" Father Juan asked smiling.

"I do not need to go to confessional anymore, Father Juan. I am just like you. I am a minister now, and I must go directly to God with my problems and any sins that I might accidentally commit." Carlotta Garcia declared confidently, looking the

Jo Hammers

40ish Catholic priest right in the eye.

"That is craziness you are speaking, Carlotta. Are you and your friends smoking something you shouldn't be?" He asked thinking she might be using marijuana.

"I am a good girl. I do not smoke, drink, or do anything that might send me to your confessional." She shot back. "I had a sore throat the last time after going to your confessional. Forcing me to say 'Hail Mary' seventy five times was unreasonable for my sin of kicking my brother Pablo in church and making him scream. He deserved the kick. He had just pinched me when mama wasn't looking."

"Your mother will see to it that you return to confessional. It will be more than fifty 'Hail Mary's I will make you say for daring to say you are now like me and that you don't need to come to me to confess anymore."

"I am a holiness, Pentecostal, Protestant minister now, and I answer directly to God . . . not you!" She replied in a defiant firm voice.

"Women cannot be priests." He shot back in an annoyed voice. "Furthermore, even I must go to confessional when needed. Father Paul from the town over hears me."

"You don't confess and talk directly to God?" She asked with a surprised look on her face.

"Do not insult me, Carlotta. I follow rules concerning confessions, just like every other member of the Catholic Church. I hear from God when one of the other fathers hears my confession and tells me what to do for penance. Afterward I am forgiven."

"I am sorry you have to have someone else hear from God for you, Father Juan. Have you been a bad boy? I have tried to be a good girl. Maybe God likes me better. He speaks to me."

"You insolent little . . . ," Father Juan replied, stopping short of scolding her in not so nice words. He bit his tongue for a moment. Coming from a street kid background, he still had the tendency to want to use certain cuss words when his buttons were pushed.

"Insolent little what . . . ?" She asked with a smirk on her face, seeing she had got the best of him. She was thirteen and still acted like one at times, even if she was called to preach.

"Women cannot be priests." He returned sternly giving her his version of a Catholic holy evil eye. He often used the eye to make children sit still and be quiet in services.

"Your God is a male chauvinist, Father Juan. My God likes boys and girls. He calls both to preach and serve him. My God and Holy Ghost speak directly to me. I do not need to get my father to drive me seventy fifty miles to the next town to get a message from another priest. My God likes Sandy Soil Texas and me."

"You are at the point of blaspheming, Carlotta. Stop this nonsense now!" He shot back. He wasn't used to those in his parish questioning or back talking to him.

"I had a vision, Father Juan. In it, I saw Jesus. He told me that the two churches here in Sandy Soil, Texas have deaf ears to him. How many 'Hail Marys' are you going to have to say for not hearing him?" She shot back.

"I am going to talk to your mother about your insolence, Carlotta."

"What have you done Father Juan to make God not hear you?" Carlotta asked, continuing while ignoring the priest's mad eyes staring at her. She was not frightened of him.

"I have done nothing, Carlotta. How dare you say such a thing to me! I have been to seminary and have been a priest for years. I am God's chosen, not you. God doesn't call women to be anything but nuns. You are a lesser vessel in his sight." He shot back in pure annoyance, trying to get even with her. She was pushing all of his buttons. He was totally at the point of cussing.

"The lesser vessel is the one who does not hear directly from God!" She shot back, raising one eyebrow and giving him her version of the eye.

Exasperated and totally pissed off, Father Juan shot back, "You are just a thirteen year old child. If you were older, I would put your name on God's list to be excommunicated from our Holy Catholic Church. Keep saying the things you are saying, and I will see that you get ex communicated in spite of your age. Our holy Catholic Church does not put up with Protestant non-sense. Now, get out of my church, Carlotta. Go home! When you are ready for confessional, you may return." Father Juan stated in a raised, stern, 'holier than thou' voice.

"You may throw me out of this, your church, but your God is not my god. Mine speaks directly to me and he has called me to preach. He has also told me to build a church right smack dab in the center between your Catholic Church and the God Assembly. He has told me to build it right smack dab in the middle of my mama's flower bed, the one you sprinkled holy water on so flowers would grow."

"Your mother is a devout Catholic, Carlotta. She will die before she will let you build a protestant church on her patch of ground that she grows flowers on for our church. Keep this talk up and I will go straight to your mother and tell her that I am going to throw you out of the church and that you will die and go to a pit of fire that will consume you forever. Don't mess with me Carlotta." Father Juan stated, totally pissed off at the mouthy girl.

"You have shown me your true colors, Father Juan. Now, I will show you God's colors." Carlotta replied.

Carlotta's big toe started to tingle and Holy Ghost goose bumps started to run up her leg and then up her spine. She raised her right hand to heaven. As her whole body quivered, she began to speak in Holy Ghost tongues. Then she suddenly spoke with a voice that was not hers. The voice said, "Touch not my anointed, and do my prophetess no harm. Because you have chosen to speak words of harm toward her, you will lie flat till you repent in her altar. Thus says the Lord God Almighty."

Father Juan backed up in shock, fearing the shaking and quivering girl, not to mention the husky, non female voice that had just spoken thru her that was not hers.

After a moment of Holy Ghost unknown tongue praying and the voice coming forth, Carlotta lowered her right hand and pointed it at the priest.

Now, seriously frightened of the girl that he felt had to be demon possessed, Father Juan backed up quickly, roughly plunging into a tall, pedestal, bird bath type looking vessel that held holy water. It immediately tipped over and all the holy water splashed onto the floor. Off balance, from backing into it, he fell backwards onto the floor.

Laughing in the Holy Ghost, Carlotta began to dance in the spirit and twirl in circles in the foyer of the Catholic Church.

As she did so, Father Juan jumped up. He felt he needed to run and put distance between him and what he considered to be a demon possessed girl. Losing his balance again, he slipped in the spilt holy water, fell flat of his back, and lay groaning in pain as Carlotta threw her right hand in the air and shouted, "Hallelujah!"

Walking out of the church, Carlotta did not help the sprawled priest up. However, just as she was about to slip out of the massive entry door, she turned and pointed her finger at the frightened priest saying, "God got you didn't he?"

Carlotta was called of God, but she was also a thirteen year old kid who laughed when others burped, cut winds, or tripped and fell. Carlotta had a thirteen year old child moment.

Father Juan bit his tongue, as he lay helpless and in pain in the spilt holy water on the floor. He didn't feel it would be a wise thing to argue any further with the girl, especially since he was flat of his back and not capable of getting up to defend himself if the demon possessed girl attacked him. He began to yell for help, hoping one of the nuns would hear him and come to his rescue. He literally could not get up. He was flat of his back, just as the voice had said.

CHAPTER FIVE

The Pompoous Reverend Pierce

Outside the church, Carlotta started walking back toward her home on the sandy dirt road, to face her mother. Headed toward her walking on the same road was the pastor of the God Assembly church, Reverend Pierce. He was not Hispanic like Carlotta. His skin was lily white. The protestant reverend carried an enormous umbrella and wore a huge straw hat to keep his lily white face and body from sun burning.

"Good morning, Carlotta." He greeted her, stopping to chat for a moment. He closed and put down his umbrella for a moment. "What is up?"

"What is up is that I have had a recent 'God experience.'" She replied all smiles.

"That is great, Carlotta." He replied. "Tell me more."

"Mama let me go down to that Pentecostal lady's tent revival last week; that was set up next to the market. All my friends were going. We just wanted to sit on the back rows, socialize, and watch the odd things the Pentecostals do. My friends all laughed and cut up during service. I did not. I had a God experience, Reverend Pierce. God filled me with the Holy Ghost and then called me to preach and build a church. I am going to pastor a church." Carlotta replied.

Reverend Pierced coughed and then cleared his throat before speaking. "Carlotta, I am an ordained, licensed minister with the God Assemblies. I do not hang out with renegade, unlicensed, Pentecostals; especially misled women, who have no male overseers to guide them, like the lady tent evangelist. Furthermore, women are not called by God to preach. A woman's place is at home as a mother and some man's wife. The most a woman can do in church is to be a pianist or Sunday school teacher. As a licensed, recognized minister, I do not hang out with renegade Pentecostal male preachers, much less female ones. I did not attend the tent meeting because of the fact that a renegade, misled woman was holding it. I also told my members they were not to attend."

"That is funny . . . "Carlotta replied looking the Protestant minister directly in the eye. "My Catholic priest says he doesn't hang out with you for the same reason. He calls you a Protestant renegade. He says long ago you Protestants were excommunicated from the Catholic Church for doctrinal heresies."

Rev. Pierce coughed and turned an instant shade of red like his lily white skin was suddenly sun burned. "Go on," he replied in an annoyed voice, thinking she would tell him more about the priest who was speaking so badly of him.

Carlotta took his words as meaning to tell him more about the lady tent evangelist and the meeting.

"The lady evangelist spoke and as she did the Holy Ghost come upon her. She quivered and shook as she spoke. As she did so, I could see white spirits flying all about in the tent and they were touching people. One touched me. It was as though I had stuck my finger in an electric socket. The Lady evangelist spoke about the Holy Ghost and fire that would enter you, fill you up, guide you, speak to you, and set your feet a dancing. She said that all you had to do was get into her prayer line to receive. I made a run for her line." Carlotta replied.

"Did you say you danced?" Reverend Pierce asked in a huff.

"I have always dreamed of being a dancer. My friend Wendy at school takes ballet. I went down and got in her prayer line and asked to be made a dancer. I got way more than I went down for, Reverend Pierce. The lady evangelist slapped her quivering hand on my head and I went to dancing, spinning in circles, and speaking in a language I did not know. Then, I saw Jesus. He said to me, "Build a church, Carlotta. Preach my gospel."

"Now, Carlotta," Reverend Pierce stated in a huff. "Dancing is a sin. Furthermore, women cannot be ministers or pastors. Only men can be ministers, evangelists, and pastors. You can be called to be a Sunday school teacher, a worker in the church kitchen, or a pianist. That is all.

God does not call women to be ministers. Man is above and head of woman. Women are to be wives for men and, and mothers to children. A woman's place is in the home. It is only men that God calls to the ministry."

"Let us both pray, Reverend Pierce. I will lift my hand to heaven. You do the same. I will call on my God and Holy Ghost to let a sign fall showing which of us is right. If my calling is true, his wrath will fall from the sky on you. If you are right, God's wrath will fall from the sky on me."

"Don't tempt God, Carlotta." He shot back.

"I am tempting God, Reverend Pierce." She stated as her right big toe started to tingle and tap. As a shiver ran up her body, she raised her thirteen year old right hand to the heavens and began to pray in tongues. After praying in tongues, she opened her eyes, looked into the heavens, and said, "If I be a woman called of God to preach, let your wrath fall now on Reverend Pierce's head." She then began to dance and spin in circles.

Putting his umbrella down on the ground, and removing his huge straw hat, Rev. Pierce turned his head and eyes upward toward the blue, cloudless, desert sky with a smirk on his face, sure in himself that he had made his point. After all, this was a desert area and it rarely rained. He had her.

"I don't see any rain clouds!" He stated in a 'know it all' condescending voice glancing at Carlotta who was lost in the Spirit of God.

Looking back up with intentions of saying further things to destroy the girl's belief that she was called to preach, he once more eyed the blue sky. As he looked up, with his lily white face unprotected, the biggest black crow ever seen in the area flew over and unloaded his belly load of crap. Splat went the crap on the center of Rev. Pierce's lily white forehead. Then the bird crap mess proceeded to run down in a liquid form into his eyes, down his nose, and across his lips. He gagged, spit, coughed, cleared his throat and wiped frantically with his hands to clear his sight. It was as though someone had turned over a huge bowl of soupy chili over his head.

"It is your turn, Reverend Pierce. Are you ready to show me your power?" Carlotta asked opening her eyes to face the male chauvinist minister.

"Get out of my way!" he stated in a huff, as he grabbed his umbrella and turned to return in the direction he came from to bathe and get the stinking crap off of himself. With every breath, he wanted to throw up from the stench.

Watching the 'Bird Crap' praying event from her little home's front porch (that faced the sandy soil dirt road), was an aging widow named Sandy Summer Storm. She had laughingly witnessed the "God's wrath moment' duel between Carlotta and the Reverend Pierce. Sandy Summer Storm was not Catholic, or Protestant. She was Native American and believed in a Great White Spirit, Kachina, and a Mystical White Buffalo Woman. Even though she had laughed while watching the huge crow crap on Reverend Pierce, she had not laughed at Carlotta. She was drawn to the strange shaking, quivering, and the spinning in circles dancing of Carlotta. She remembered the days when she was a child when her tribe's medicine men did rain dances, calling on the Gods to come down. She wondered if Carlotta wasn't partly Native American. She definitely had displayed the rain dance gift that she saw exhibited by her tribe's medicine men when she was very young.

Thanks to the 'porch sitting' widow named Sandy Summer Storm, word in the little town spread quickly about Carlotta's circle dancing and how her God sent a huge black crow to crap on her enemy.

CHAPTER SIX

Two or Three in my Name

Carlotta stood at the edge of her mother's flower bed, wondering how she was going to come up with the money to build a church and buy pews for it. She also wondered how she was going to get her mother to agree to the project, and let her have the flower garden land. The flowers would all have to go for a cement floor to be poured. As she was contemplating the situation, Edith White Suit came walking down the road barefoot. She stopped at the rickety, mesquite branch fence to chat for a moment. Carlotta ran to the fence to greet her.

"What is on your mind, Carlotta? You look so serious." Edith stated, wading into conversation.

"Do you remember when I knocked the bee from your hair in the tent meeting?"

"Yes, Carlotta. Why do you ask?" replied Edith White Suit, as wisps of her red hair moved gently in a breeze that seemed to only be blowing on her.

"Do you remember me telling you that I wished for God to give me the gift of dance?"

"Yes, I remember." Edith replied all smiles.

"My ballet friend Wendy at school has dumped me as her best friend. She says my Holy Ghost dancing is an embarrassment to her. Also, my brother, Pablo, says I am devil possessed. I just don't understand why my friends and family do not see what a wonderful experience it is to know the Holy Ghost. Even my mother does not see the wonderful gift from God that has been given me. All she thinks about is her flowers."

"Do you remember who you were friends with when you were in Kindergarten?" Edith White Suit asked.

"Millie, the daughter of the truck driver that lives a couple of miles from here, was my friend. Why do you ask?"

"Is she your friend now?"

"No. . . She moved away. Wendy replaced her and was my friend till just recently."

"Friends, Carlotta, come and go on your path. New ones come along to support you as you grow, mature, and take new forks in the road on your spiritual journey. Millie went away and Wendy came into your life. Now, it is time for Wendy to go away and someone new to come into your life again. God will send you a new friend to walk every fork in the road that you take as your ministry and life moves forward. One day, you will look back and Wendy will be like your kindergarten friend, Millie, just a memory."

"I understand, Edith White Suit." Carlotta replied.

"Is there anything else you would like to chat about?" Edith asked.

"I see things, Edith White Suit, things that I do not understand why I see them."

"Tell me about the things you see, Carlotta."

"When I think about God, Jesus, and the Holy Ghost, my right foot's toe just can't contain itself. It dance's in the spirit, whether I wish it to or not. When the Holy Ghost gets a hold of me, and I am speaking the unknown tongue words he wants me to say, I see visions of who needs what from God. As I was standing looking at my mother's flower garden, I suddenly saw my brother Pablo needing his mouth and lungs washed out with a bar of soap. He was cussing and smoking cigarettes behind the market."

"God is giving you the Word of Knowledge, Carlotta. You must be able to see what the need of a person is, before you can pray for deliverance for that individual. The soap represents the power of the Holy Ghost." Edit White Suit stated. "Pray for your little brother. Prayer will draw him to you. You have the power to cleanse him from his behind the market dark ways."

"Thank you for those words, Edith White Suit. I have wondered about what I see and what I am to do about what I see."

Is there anything else you would like to talk about? Edith asked.

"What am I going to do, Edith White Suit? God has told me to stand in my mother's flower garden patch and preach my first sermon this coming Sunday. You know how my mother Rosa becomes a screeching, wild, ban chi woman when anyone steps near her flower bed. I fear she might chase someone who has come to listen to me with her broom, or maybe even a rake. When she is mad, she is no one to mess with. I run from her broom. My dogs run from her broom. What am I going to do?"

"To start with, on Sunday morning before your mother awakens, hide her broom and rake. All she will have left to chase you and your new church members with will be her fly swatter."

Carlotta snickered. She was only thirteen.

"Concerning my church, Edith White Suit, how do I get my mother to let me have the flower garden patch of land to build my church on. Also, where do I get the money to build my church and buy benches for the inside?"

"How many people does it take to make a church?" Edith White Suit asked in reply, as she stood up straight and quit leaning on the rickety Mesquite branch fence.

"The God Assembly down the road has thirty or so members. The Catholic Church where mama goes for mass has at least a hundred. I suppose I will need thirty or a hundred seats, money for concrete for a floor, and materials to build a small building with." Carlotta replied, trying to assess her needs in her head.

"A church is not concrete, sticks, stones, or pews, Carlotta. Listen closely to what I am about to tell you. The bible says that where two or three are gathered together in God's name, he will be in the midst. All you need to be a church in God's sight is for two or three people to gather together."

"Do you mean that I could stand in the middle of a dirt road with two or three believers and that would become a church in that moment, and that God would come down and walk with us?"

"Yes." Edith White Suit answered simply.

"I just want to be sure I am clear on what you are telling me, Edith White Suit. If I have two or three friends at school, who choose to follow Christ like me, we can meet in the girl's restroom and that God will come down and walk amongst us there and for that moment, the girl's restroom will become a church also?"

"Yes, Carlotta. God does not come down to walk in fancy churches with annexes and expensive stained glass windows. God comes down when two or three are gathered in his name. Manmade buildings have nothing to do with it."

"Wait till I tell my friend Wendy about this. Boys aren't allowed in the girl's restroom. If I hold services there during recess, the first boy ever will have free access to the girl's room. Christ will be allowed to enter and walk amongst us there."

This time it was Edith White Suit's turn to snicker. Although Carlotta was called, she was still just thirteen and thought things out accordingly.

Suddenly, Carlotta's dancing toe started to tap. As she began to quiver and shake in the Holy Ghost, she repeated back to Edith White Suit her perception of what Edith had told her.

"All I need to start a church is for two or three people to gather. I will need only three chairs, just in case those coming and gathering are elderly. All others coming can stand, because pews do not make a church. When we meet, God will come down and walk amongst us."

"You've got it, Carlotta. Set up two or three chairs for the elderly in your mother's flower bed. When you have two or three people coming to fill those chairs, God will come down. At that point, you have built a church."

"Thank you, Edith White Suit. I will set up my three chairs church in the middle of mama's flower bed this Sunday." stated Carlotta in deep thought. She then proceeded to shiver and then dance uncontrollably in the Holy Ghost.

Edith White Suit slipped away into the sunlight of the morning, leaving Carlotta to be alone with her God and her new revelation.

CHAPTER SEVEN

Holy Water

Sunday morning came and Rosa Garcia woke up Benita and Pablo to get ready for early mass. Hidalgo had risen early to go hunting in the desert for a Jack rabbit for their noon meal. Carlotta lay in her bed with eyes closed, hoping her mother would not make her get up to go to mass. She needed the early morning hours to set up her first church.

Carlotta's mother did not wake her or shake her. Carlotta was sure that her mother feared that she would display one of what her mother called 'Holy Ghost fits' during mass. Rosa had made it very clear to Carlotta that she was embarrassed at having a daughter that had suddenly gone mad and was willingly possessed by a Protestant Holy Ghost demon.

Carlotta waited patiently in her bed, pretending that she was asleep. She waited unmoving for them to leave. When Carlotta heard them leave the yard making morning talk, Carlotta threw her sheet off and sprung from her bed. She had a church to build, a sermon to preach, and just a short time, one hour, to do it. Carlotta had slept in her clothes, fully knowing what a short time span she would have while her family went to mass. Catholic Mass at her church only lasted an hour. That would not give her much time to do what she needed to do.

On the front porch of Carlotta's tiny adobe home, sat three short, woven seat peasant chairs. Running from her house, she grabbed one by its slat back and made a bee line for her mother's flower bed. Before stepping into the flowers, Carlotta raised one hand to heaven and said, "Mama's flowers are in your keeping God. If she gets mad, you handle it."

Having prayed, Carlotta tip toed thru the flowers and placed the first little porch chair facing where she was going to be standing and speaking. Afterward, she made a second quick trip to the porch and retrieved the other two chairs. Hurriedly, she ran and placed them next to the first, forming a short little row. Flowers in the garden were high as the seats.

The morning was warm. Carlotta wiped perspiration from her forehead. For a brief moment, she paused to admire her single row of three chairs. Then she had a panic moment. She wondered if she would need holy water to swing back and forth sprinkling the church and the congregation during her services. Father Juan, her family's Catholic priest, did it every week. Having been reared Catholic Carlotta's knowledge of how a church service was to be conducted was a mixture of tent meeting service order and the traditions of the Catholic Church. The Catholic side of her wondered if she needed holy water for her first service.

As Carlotta was pondering the thought, Edith White Suit came walking up the road in front of the Garcia's property. Carlotta waved and motioned for her to stop. She then ran speedily to the front fence in hopes Edith White Suit would have the answer.

"Edith White Suit . . . Edith White Suit . . . wait! I need advice."

Edith slowed her pace and walked up to the Garcia's fence and leaned waiting for Carlotta to reach her and speak.

"I see you have built your church this morning!" Edith stated eyeing the three chairs that set in the middle of Rosa Garcia's flower bed.

"Yes . . . I am all ready to preach my first sermon, just as soon as God sends someone to sit in the three chairs. However, I have a question of most importance that I need an answer for."

"What would that question be Reverend Carlotta, called one of God?"

"Should my church be sanctified with holy water, like Father Juan does weekly to his church?"

Edith White Suit bit her lip and smiled. "There is holy water, Carlotta, and then there is spiritual holy water that you cannot see with human eyes, drink with human lips, or feel its touch on your human brow when it falls on you. Father Juan's holy water can be seen in the vessel he carries it in, and can be seen wet when sprinkled on skin or an object. Spiritual holy water comes down from heaven. It is the spiritual holy water that you must sanctify your new church with. It will fall like invisible rain. You will be the vessel that sprinkles it on everyone as you lay hands on those who come to you."

"Oh . . . ! " Carlotta said as a light bulb seemingly turned on inside of her as though she had received a great revelation.

"When the Holy Ghost starts your toe to tapping, you are entering the Land of Spirit, Carlotta. It is the anointing in the Land of Spirit that is the holy water of God. Remember the night you were called to preach in the tent meeting service?" Edith questioned.

"How could I ever forget, Edith White Suit? It was my personal God moment."

"Remember how you felt when the Holy Ghost power descended on you and you began to dance and speak in tongues?"

"It just washed over me, Edith White Suit."

"The washing over you, Carlotta, is spiritual rain. It is water that human eyes cannot see. Your priest's holy water is just tap water, human drinking water. It can be seen. God's holy water rain cannot be seen."

"So, holy water is like God. You can't see God, but he is there. You can't see spiritual holy water with human eyes, yet it is there. I understand, Edith White Suit."

"You are one smart God girl." Edith replied.

"I have one more question, Edith White Suit." Carlotta stated with a twinkle in her eye.

"What is your question?" Edith asked.

"Do you think the Holy Ghost's holy rain could make the legs on my three church chairs dance like I do, when it falls and washes over them and those seated in them?"

Edith broke out in laughter. Regaining her composure, she said, "With God, all things are possible, Carlotta."

"Thank you, Edith White Suit for explaining holy water to me." Carlotta stated with a satisfied look on her face. "I will pray and anoint my chairs with spiritual holy water from the heavens. I want my chairs to dance if it is God's will."

"It is not just chairs that you will need to anoint with holy water, Carlotta. You must anoint every member of your new church. All who are anointed by you with Holy Spirit water will be called into God's service."

"Anoint with holy spiritual rain water and call them forth. I will do it, Edith White Suit." Carlotta answered.

Edith White Suit was a glorious looking human being. She always wore a high neck, long sleeved, long skirted white suit that was spotless, and she always walked barefoot. Edith was not an old woman. She looked to be about 30. Her wavy red hair was long, and wisps of it blew gently when a breeze was moving about. However, her hair never looked uncombed or windblown.

"Thank you Edith White Suit. I will go now and anoint my chairs with holy water that cannot be seen with human eyes. With that said, Carlotta turned and made a run for her mother's flower garden that was now her first church.

Carlotta turned for a moment to glance back at Edith White Suit and wave. The barefoot woman in a white suit was gone.

Returning to her chairs in the flower patch, Carlotta closed her eyes to let God make him-self manifest and anoint her chairs and flower garden church floor with spiritual waters. As she did, her right big toe started to tap. She quickly placed her hand palm down on the chairs one by one and let the spirit flow. After anointing the third, she reached down and touched the sandy soil beneath the flowers blessing it with heaven's spiritual holy water. Then she stood, raised her right hand toward heaven, shivered, shook, spoke in unknown tongues, and then shouted,

"Hallelujah!" Opening her eyes, she prepared to greet whoever God would send to fill her three chairs for her first service.

To her surprise, the widow named Sandy Summer Storm was seated in one of her three anointed chairs. She was all decked out in purple beaded Native American ceremony clothes and moccasins. Her hair was braided down the back with black crow feathers in the weave. She wore so much turquoise jewelry on her fingers, wrists, ears, and neck, that it made her look like a walking jewelry store.

Native American widow, Sandy Summer Storm was born during a sand storm that blew thru the southwest desert eighty or so years before. Local inhabitants of the little one horse Texas town just called her Sandy.

Pleased as punch to have her first chair filled with a sitter, Carlotta shook Sandy's hand like they did at the Pentecostal tent meeting, before services.

"Welcome, Sandy Summer Storm. I know that God has sent you to listen to my first sermon. Welcome in the name of God, Jesus Christ, and the Holy Ghost."

"I have journeyed here to see if my rain dancing 'Great White Spirit' is your Holy Ghost dancing God." Sandy Summer Storm returned.

"My Holy Ghost is indeed a dancer." stated Carlotta all smiles. "My Holy Ghost is my God's voice, his mouthpiece on Earth."

"My Great White Spirit speaks with thunder." Sandy returned.

"So does my God at times." Carlotta replied.

"I also wish to know if you are a Crow rain dancer. I saw you dance in the road in front of my house and call down a great black crow to relieve itself on the Reverend Pierce who was denying your woman minister calling. I was watching and listening from my rocker on my front porch. When I was a very little girl, our medicine men danced in circles and chanted words I did not understand. I was about six back then. I have not seen rain dancing in over thirty years. My entire tribe of friends and family are dead. My Native American mother and father have been crossed over to the happy hunting ground for many years of moons. My mother would be over a hundred now if she were alive. This ceremonial dance dress and moccasins that I am wearing were hers. She wore them to rain dance in when I was a child."

"I am sorry about the death of your tribe and the loss of your parents." Carlotta stated with all seriousness. However, God has a family, a tribe that you can belong to for all your days on Earth. I would be much pleased if you would become a member of my new three chair church tribe, Sandy Summer Storm. You are welcome to dance with me, my God, my Holy Ghost, and Your Great White Spirit which I am sure is the same as my God."

"Thank you, Carlotta." Sandy returned with a look of sunshine entering her facial expression. "How shall I dance when the dancing starts, like you or like the crow medicine men I remember?"

"My Holy Ghost makes me dance in circles that I cannot control. You are welcome to dance with me, in whatever way you feel led to. I once dreamed of dancing the white man's ballet dance. Now, I dance a greater dance, that of the Holy Ghost. He has made a circle and spinning dancer out of me. Maybe it is his will to make us both medicine women that circle rain dance together."

"I need a sign, Carlotta, if I am to join your tribe. I am too old to go into the desert on a vision quest and ask if I am to join you. "

"What sign do you wish, Sandy Summer Storm?"

"If you can medicine woman dance and make it rain this morning, and only on this flower garden, I will join your Holy Ghost church tribe." Sandy replied. "I need a sign that you are a true medicine woman."

Carlotta smiled. "My God's Holy Ghost can do anything. When I pray, after my sermon, do you also wish that the rain will fall on you?"

"Let it fall on just this garden patch of flowers, Carlotta. I have on my mother's ceremony dance dress. It is very old and fragile."

"How about your soul, Sandy Summer Storm . . . do you wish my Holy Ghost rain to fall on it along with the natural rain on this garden of flowers?"

"Yes, I like your Holy Ghost. Let it fall on my soul. It is also okay for the natural rain to fall on my head and hands, just not my dress and moccasins."

Carlotta snickered. She felt inside her that God was sending her new friends to replace Wendy and the other girls at school. This new friend was much . . . very much older than her. Sandy Summer Storm was over eighty.

"One more thing, before you speak and pray, medicine woman Carlotta . . . be sure to pray for rain and not bird crap."

"I will pray for blessings this morning, not wrath." Carlotta replied all smiles.

Suddenly, Carlotta's big toe wanted to tap and dance. As she headed for a spot in the front of the chairs to deliver her first sermon, the two Garcia family dogs made a run into the flower patch and each leaped up into one of the other two short peasant chairs and sat in them. Carlotta was pleased. Her three chairs were full.

CHAPTER EIGHT

The Rain Dance

As Carlotta began to speak, she told the story of how she went down to the tent meeting to socialize with her friends and how God had used the lady tent evangelist to pray for her and how the Holy Ghost came upon her and made her speak in tongues, spin in circles, and dance lost in the Holy Ghost.

After telling her story for a sermon, Carlotta closed her first service by inviting anyone who needed something from God to come forward, and that she would pray for them like the lady tent evangelist had prayed for her.

The two family dogs jumped out of their two chairs and made their way to where Carlotta stood and sat down behind her. Then, Sandy Summer Storm stood and walked to where Carlotta stood.

"What would you have of our Great White Spirit God and the Holy Ghost, Sandy Summer Storm?" Carlotta asked, as they stood in the Sunday morning sunshine amongst her mother's flowers.

Jo Hammers

"I want a sign from my Great White Spirit that you are a true medicine woman and rain dancer. If your God is my Great White Spirit, I wish him to rain on this flower patch, right here where we stand, but not get my very old and treasured ceremony dress wet."

"Raise your hands, Sandy Summer Storm." Carlotta told her as her big toe started to tap. She then looked up into the cloudless sky and started to pray. "It is time God to bless those who have come to hear about you, Jesus, and the Holy Ghost. I ask a special blessing and miracle gift to fall on this special Native American woman that wishes to know you as real. As I begin to speak in tongues and dance, I am asking you to fill her with the Holy Ghost. Make her speak in tongues and rain dance in Holy Ghost circles like me!" stated Carlotta with all emphasis and seriousness. "Also, I ask for a literal outburst of rain to fall on every flower in this garden, but that not a drop fall on Sandy's very old ceremony dress as a sign to her."

Then, Carlotta started to feel the Holy Ghost that was tapping in her big right toe as it moved up her leg up her body and into her arms that she raised to heaven. Suddenly she spoke in unknown tongues and then started to shake and shiver in the Holy Ghost anointing. "Let the rain fall, God!" she yelled, and then closing her eyes she started to dance around her three chairs in unending, spinning circles; speaking in tongues, chanting in tongues, and totally lost in the spirit.

Sandy Summer Storm raised her arms and suddenly looked like a bird that was about to take flight with raised arm like wings. The fringe on her mother's ceremony dress sleeves floated and moved as she waved her arms up and down. As she did, the Holy Ghost fell on her and she flew round and round Carlotta's three chairs, following Carlotta. Sandy Summer Storm was over 80 years old, yet she Holy Ghost rain danced with ease. As she circled and danced seemingly on the wind behind Carlotta, she began to chant in Holy Ghost tongues. Round and round the three chairs danced the two Holy Ghost filled women.

Suddenly, out of nowhere, a cloud the size of a bed sheet appeared over the three chairs and the two dancers. Then the cloud began to spit sprinkles of physical rain. When the sprinkles fell all around them, the two women danced faster and with laughter in the Holy Ghost. Then the cloud burst and water poured down, soaking Carlotta, the flower patch, the chairs, and the dogs, but not one drop fell on the special ceremony dress. Sandy Summer Storm's hair, face, and hands were soaked. However not a drop of fallen rain dripped onto the dress. The rain fell for ten minutes and then quit. Sandy Summer Storm was pleased that Carlotta's God was real and her Great White Spirit.

While Carlotta was dismissing service, Sandy Summer Storm looked out toward the road and saw Edith White Suit standing, watching, and waving at her. She raised her eighty year old hand and waved back. Sandy wondered if it was possible that Edith White Suit was her White Buffalo Woman.

As Carlotta was picking up one of her mother's porch chairs by its back, to return it to the front porch, a screeching voice pierced the air.

"Carlotta!" yelled Rosa Garcia in an extremely mad tone. "I am going to beat your back side with my broom Carlotta, just as soon as I can walk again. I saw you and those dogs and that dancing Indian in my flowers!"

Rosa Garcia was leaning against her house's porch. She had been in too much pain to run with her broom to chase Carlotta, the dogs, and Sandy Summer Storm out of her flowers. Rosa Garcia had tripped, when leaving her Catholic Church, on the outside steps. She had sprained both of her ankles so badly that she had to be brought home in the back of a pickup owned by one of the other Parish members. Just as God had caused a crow to fly over and get the Reverend Pierce, God had let his wrath fall on Rosa in a manner that kept her from interfering with Carlotta's first church service.

CHAPTER NINE

Casting Out a Demon

From that day forward, Rosa Garcia was unable to walk down and run people and animals from her flower garden, although she did plenty of yelling from a distance. Carlotta Garcia set up her three chair church in the middle of the flower garden every Sunday for the summer. Sandy Summer Storm became her first Holy Ghost filled member.

For about the first three weeks, Pastor Carlotta spoke and led her tiny flock of one elderly woman and two family dogs. Then, one Sunday morning, a fortyish looking nun, in a long flowing black habit, walked thru the front gate and to the three chairs in the flower bed. She quietly seated herself next to Sandy Summer Storm. Carlotta greeted her with a hand shake, just as she had Sandy on her first morning in the three chair church.

"Good morning, Sister Margaret," Carlotta greeted her. "Welcome to God's house."

Sister Margaret was one of two nuns who lived in the back of the Catholic Church.

"Good morning Carlotta. I have come to ask if your God is in the healing business this morning. " She stated simply in a voice of reverence. "The God I have been faithful to my whole life, seems to be turning a deaf ear to me now in my time of need. I need someone to pray for healing for me. My prayers are not getting thru."

Carlotta looked down at her own hand. She had nicked one of her fingers earlier in the morning when she was peeling and cutting an avocado to eat before she started to set up her church. She had a fresh bloody cut about a half inch long.

"The lady evangelist at the spring, Pentecostal tent meeting prayed for the sick, Sister Mary Margaret. I have not paid much attention to those in need of healing till now, because I am rarely ill. However, this morning I am in need of a healing also." She stated, holding out her cut finger for the nun to see. "If you will be seated and listen to my morning sermon, afterward I will ask God to send his Holy Ghost down to heal you and me. It is my opinion that my God and his Holy Ghost are healers and capable of anything."

"I do not understand your Pentecostal Holy Ghost, Carlotta. However, I am willing to be open minded and let him speak to me and heal me. I am dying, Carlotta. Two months ago, I was diagnosed with un-operable breast cancer. I have a lump in my breast the size of a goose egg. I do not wish to die yet, Carlotta. In my head I hear a voice calling me to preach the gospel. I don't know how that can be when only priests in our church can be ministers. Also, why would I be dying if I am supposed to go and preach? I cannot go to Father Juan with this. He will excommunicate me. He is really mad right now over you converting to be a Pentecostal. He warned our parish last week that anyone attending even one of your flower garden meetings will be thrown out of the Catholic Church."

"God's church is not a building or a denomination, Sister Margaret. It is where two or three people are gathered together in his name and call upon him to come down and walk with them. In all truth, God's church is a walking one."

"I am indeed walking this morning, Carlotta. I walked out on the other nun as we were preparing for morning service. In just a matter of weeks I will be on my death bed. I have cared for and watched women die with breast cancer, Carlotta. It is not a pretty death."

"What would you do for God, if I pray and he sends down the Holy Ghost to heal you?" Carlotta asked, while at the same time considering what she would do for God if he healed her finger in a miraculous fashion.

"I will give up my Catholic faith and become a member of the church where God does come down to heal and speak. I have never heard the voice of God or seen a miracle done in my years of church service. I have seen a lot of parish members die from diseases, and be excommunicated for seeking miracles and healing elsewhere. Now, it is my time to face death. I am willing to give up everything to be healed. I want to hear God's voice, not the voice of Father Juan in a confessional."

Carlotta turned to Sandy Summer Storm. "Are you prepared to Holy Ghost Dance for healing miracles after I speak?"

"I am ready Great White Spirit medicine woman. Your God and your Holy Ghost have filled me with tongues and spiritual rain dancing. Our Holy Ghost and shared Great White Spirit are capable of healing that which cannot be healed. I will rain dance with you for healing, Carlotta, called one of God.

So, Carlotta once more stood in front of the three chairs and spoke of how she had gone down to the tent meeting and was filled with the Holy Ghost, spoke in tongues, and danced in the spirit. This time she added the story of the miracle rain that had fallen when Sandy Summer Storm had attended her first service. Then it was time to call forth those in need. She waited till her big toe started to tingle with dance before doing so.

"Come forth now for the laying on of hands and the asking of miracles from God." She stated raising her right hand into the air and shivering in the presence of the God and the Holy Ghost.

Sister Margaret, the 40 year old nun, rose from her chair and stepped forward amongst the flowers to stand before Carlotta.

"What do you have need of Sister Mary? The need must be spoken." She stated.

"I wish to be healed of a goose egg size lump in my breast. Cancer is eating me alive. I do not feel that my mission on Earth is completed, that the cancer is the devil, and he is trying to prevent me from doing what I know that I am suppose to be doing. I am called to leave the Catholic Church and to become a woman minister."

"Raise your hands to heaven, Sister Margaret." Carlotta instructed. "When the Holy Ghost comes upon me, I will touch your head with my anointed hand. When the power hits me and I begin to quiver and shake, it is God doing his business." stated thirteen year old Carlotta.

"I understand," stated Sister Margaret as she stood in her long black habit and raised both her pale white hands to heaven.

Texas is known for feral wild hogs. They come out of nowhere, and will eat or attack anything. Wild hogs are mean. While Carlotta prayed, one appeared out of nowhere and was eyeing some yellow squash peelings and discards that grandmother Benita had thrown out just before dark the night before, with intentions of using the discards as fertilizer in the bottom of some holes she intended to dig to plant some new flowers along the edge of the flower bed behind Carlotta. After Rosa's accident spraining both of her ankles, Benita had taken over Rosa's chore of tending to the flowers. The feral hog gave a little squeal and started making its way toward the flower bed edge and the squash that had its attention.

Carlotta was oblivious to the wild hog, as were Sister Margaret and Sandy Summer Storm who both had their eyes closed in prayer. Carlotta raised her right hand to heaven and began to pray as she waited for the tingling in her big right toe to start moving upward, causing her to shiver and shake in the Holy Ghost.

Back, seated on her front porch with broom in hand, Rosa Garcia (with two sprained ankles that would not heal) spotted the wild hog approaching the flower patch behind Carlotta. She started screaming and swinging her broom to try to get Carlotta, Margaret, and Sandy Summer Storm's attention. Rosa knew the three women were in danger. However, the more Rosa screamed, the louder Carlotta prayed.

About that time, Pablo exited his little family's adobe house to see what his mother was screaming so frantically about. Rosa pointed to the wild hog heading for the flower patch. Pablo instantly knew what the problem was. He grabbed his mother's broom and ran for the flower garden and managed to get behind Carlotta just as the hog was about to enter the flower bed. He swung frantically at the hog causing it to back off. However, the hog was intent on tasting the yellow squash discards. It backed off a ways, but it did not go away. Pablo's forehead broke out in perspiration. He knew that feral hog was going to attack. He could see fire in its eyes.

Carlotta heard her mother and Pablo screaming. However, she ignored them. They had been yelling threats for weeks for her to get out of the flower garden on the mornings she held church. They were like the little boy who yelled wolf one time too many. When they really did need Carlotta to get out of the garden, she was not listening to them, nor was Sister Margret and Sandy Summer Storm.

With eyes closed, Carlotta prayed while remembering that her mother had threatened her with an exorcism on several occasions since she had been filled with the Holy Ghost. Still being Catholic and Pentecostal, she wondered if she should cast out the demon in Sister Margaret that was eating her alive with cancer. The answer came down to her as an inward voice saying, "Yes!"

"Great White Spirit and God of all men, I now ask you to send down your Holy Ghost and have him, thru me, cast out the cancer devil that is eating Sister Margaret alive. I ask you to send the demon flying into the nearest swine."

Carlotta had once attended her friend Wendy's Baptist Sunday school. Wendy's Sunday School teacher had told a story about Jesus casting out demons into a herd of swine and how they had ran down to the river and drowned in its water. Since Carlota did not own a Bible yet, she had to depend on what she knew from the Catholic Church, the Pentecostal Tent Meeting, and her one time morning adventure to the Baptist Sunday School in the next town over for reference.

Run, Carlotta, run!" Pablo shouted, fully knowing he needed to be running himself. His swinging the boom and screams were the only thing keeping the wild hog at bay, in his thinking.

Placing her hand on Sister Margaret's head, unbelievable power passed thru Carlotta to Sister Margaret. The black clothed nun began to quiver and shake in the Holy Ghost. Then a whooshing sound with eerie, screeching screams exited Sister Margaret and immediately flew over Carlotta and Pablo's head heading for the feral hog. However, in its screeching and screaming, it stopped mid flight when it spotted Carlotta's mother Rosa who was sitting on her porch cursing those in her flower garden. Looking back at Carlotta, the demon asked in a screech, "Which wild hog did you say?"

"Go into the nearest one," shouted Carlotta with authority.

The demon of eating cancer flew immediately thru the side of the feral hog and immediately began to gnaw and eat. The feral hog, squealed like it was on fire. It lay down in the sandy soil and rolled and rolled and rolled like it was trying to free itself from something that was burning or eating it alive. Jumping up, the feral hog ran for the desert and disappeared from sight. The demon had attacked and entered the feral hog with fire in its eyes. It had entered one of its own.

Exhausted and not knowing what was going on, perspiring Pablo asked, "What the heck?" Shaking from fright and relief, he sat down with his mother's broom in Carlotta's third chair.

After praying for Sister Margaret, Carlotta immediately felt a runaway God dance coming on her. "You are healed, Sister Margaret." She shouted and then she began to dance. As she began to spin in circles and dance around the edge of the flower garden, Sandy Summer Storm fell in behind her and proceeded to do her Native American Holy Ghost rain dance behind her. Then, as though lightning were passing thru her, Sister Margaret started jumping up and down and speaking in tongues. Then with a loud shout, she began to run in circles around the three chairs under the Power of the Holy Ghost.

Both Sister Margaret and Carlotta had been healed, although

Carlotta had not looked at her finger yet. She was lost in the power of the Holy Ghost and his dancing. Sister Margaret's goose egg size lump of cancer was gone. There was no cut on Carlotta's finger.

Pablo was somewhat afraid of Sister Margaret. She had taken him by the ear and escorted him outside the Catholic Church several times when he was interrupting services; usually on the occasions his parents did not attend with him. Sister Margaret had taken him outside and paddled him a couple of times when he was much younger. One time, his paddling was for throwing nose boogers at a visiting priest who was speaking. Another time she had fired up his backside for letting a harmless green lizard loose during service. He feared Sister Margaret.

When the power of the Holy Ghost lifted, Carlotta turned to look at her three chairs. Pablo was sitting in her third chair. She was pleased. God had filled her three chairs. Before the service ended, Sandy and Sister Margaret reseated themselves in their two chairs, with Sister Margaret seating herself next to Pablo.

Looking at Sister Margaret who was sternly eyeing him, Pablo asked, "Sister Margaret, you aren't going to paddle me for being late to Carlotta's church service, are you?"

"My paddling days are over, Pablo. I will now use the sword of the power of the Holy Ghost to set things right."

Pablo put his hand up to his throat. Would she really cut off his head with a sword if he didn't return to Carlotta's church service next week? In the moment, and in his eleven year old thinking, he decided he was not going to take any chances. He would return and sit like a good boy in his chair, next to Sister Margaret. A paddling he could deal with. However, what would he do without his head?

CHAPTER TEN

Looking for Edith White Suit

Summer was ending, but Carlotta's church was just beginning. It was growing in members every Sunday Morning, and there was standing room only. Carlotta reached a point that she felt she needed some advice as to what direction to take next with her congregation. After all, she was only thirteen.

The only person Carlotta had faith in to speak words of wisdom to her was Edith White Suit. However, she hadn't seen Edith in a couple of weeks or so. So, she decided to head down toward the God Assembly Church to see if she could locate her.

It was early in the morning, before the heat of the day set in. After finishing the breakfast dishes, Carlotta headed out to look for Edith White Suit. As she walked up and down the road hoping for an encounter with Edith, she passed in front of Sandy Summer Storm's house. She waved at Sister Margaret and Sandy Summer Storm who were sitting in rockers on the little adobe's front porch. Sister Margaret had left the Catholic Church and was now renting a room from Sandy. Her two members waved back at her.

In her search for Edith, Carlotta eventually made her way to the very small God Assembly Church. She walked around back of it, thinking there might be a small house or an apartment behind it that Edith lived in. To her surprise, there was no apartment or house, just a back door entry to the tiny one room/sanctuary church. There was no sign of Edith White Suit.

"I know . . . ," muttered Carlotta. "I will walk down to Isabel and Jose's 'Mom and Pop' market and ask if they know where Edith White Suit lives. She has to buy groceries to eat."

Isabel and Jose's little market was the only place to buy her groceries locally, if you didn't want to drive 75 miles to the next town to make purchases.

So, Carlotta left looking around at the God Assembly and continued her searching journey down the dirt road. Reaching the market, she stopped to look at the patch of desert land next to the market where the lady evangelist's tent had been set up the previous spring. She thought about the night she had attended the meeting with only the purpose of socializing with her childhood friends, but walked away at the end of the service filled with the Holy Ghost and called to preach. Her memories were Holy Ghost precious and pleasant.

After walking down memory lane, Carlotta opened the screen door to the tiny market and walked in. To her surprise, neither owner of the little market was inside. However, there was a red haired man in his early twenties leaning against the counter, seemingly waiting on something. Carlotta ignored him, due to the fact that most of the males in her life had given her a hard time about her call to preach.

The red haired man in his twenties smiled at her, but she didn't return the nicety. She did make a mental note, however, that she did like his head of wavy red hair. It was the same color as that of Edith White Suit.

Walking down a side aisle of fruits and vegetables, to avoid the red hair man, she made her way to the back screen door and peeped out in an effort to locate the storekeepers. They were out back loading cases of jugs of water into the back of a pickup truck. Carlotta did not recognize the pickup truck.

In the desert it is not uncommon for people to purchase large supplies of drinking water, due to a lack of wells and water beneath the ground. Also, most of the houses had large rain water holding tanks. Water was trucked in and the tanks filled for bathing etc. However, most people bought their drinking water in bottles and jugs.

Isabel the female storekeeper looked up and waved at Carlotta, and then half yelled, "I will be there in a moment, Carlotta. We are loading drinking water for the new God Assembly minister. He is inside. Have you met him?"

"Yes, I passed him standing at your counter," returned Carlotta in a raised voice, and at the same time rolling her eyes like a thirteen year old girl would if she was annoyed about something.

Carlotta was sure that she would be in for another round of a male trying to put her down and tell her that women couldn't be preachers, if she greeted him in any fashion.

As Carlotta stood at the backdoor waiting for the market owners to finish loading, she thought seriously about just leaving by the back door to avoid the young male minister. Then, she told herself that her God and Holy Ghost was not back door leaving cowards. So, she turned to return to the counter of the store and wait for the market's owners to get to her.

Jo Hammers

Once more the young red haired minister smiled at her. She turned her face and ignored him. She didn't have time for red headed smiling devils. She had one goal and that was to ask Isabel if she knew where Edith White Suit lived.

After a few moments, Isabel and Jose, (the mom and pop store owners) returned inside and took payment from Reverend Red Hair for his water purchase. To her relief, Carlotta was glad when the young reverend did not pursue further smiles or conversation with her. She breathed a sigh of relief.

"What can I help you with, Carlotta?" Isabel asked, leaving the young reverend and her husband Jose to their polite conversation about the weather.

"I do not need market items, this morning. I need information from you. I am trying to find Edith White Suit."

"She is probably at the cemetery. Why do you ask?" Isabel returned.

"No . . . I just passed there. She isn't visiting the grave of anyone. I usually run into Edith walking on the road between my house and here. Have you seen her this morning? It is really important that I find her."

A choking sound suddenly filled the air behind her. It was coming from the red haired preacher. Carlotta turned around to look at him, and to see why he was choking. He sounded like he had suddenly swallowed a bite of candy or maybe a gulp of soda and it went down the wrong way. As she turned about to look at the young minister, Carlotta noticed that Isabel made the sign of the cross on her body, and kissed the rosary that she always wore. Carlotta assumed that Isabel's sign of the cross was a prayer to keep the red hair man from choking to death in her store.

Jose, the male store owner, proceeded to whack the God Assembly minister on the back a few times to help him breathe. After much choking, clearing his throat, and wiping tears from his eyes, the red haired reverend regained his composure and turned to Carlotta and asked in almost a whisper, due to the hanging on effects of choking. "Did you say you see Edith White Suit walking the road outside on a regular basis?"

"Edith White Sit is a friend of mine, and yes I visit with her often when I walk on the road outside." Carlotta returned, fully annoyed that she even had to speak with the red haired protestant preacher man.

"What does Edith White Suit look like?" he managed to ask in a weak voice that was left over from choking, while at the same time grabbing Carlotta's upper right arm roughly, and holding it tightly.

Isabel interjected, "Edith is always dressed in holiness church white. She is into long sleeves, high necklines, and long skirts below her knees. Her hair is red like yours, and she always walks barefoot. Age wise, she is young like you . . . maybe thirty."

"When and where did you see her last?" he demanded, still holding firmly to Carlotta's arm.

"Let go of me, you red haired devil. How dare you to touch me, my God, and Holy Ghost within. Back off or I will call my Holy Ghost to come forth to remove your hand from me, as well as you from my presence."

Isabel noticed that Carlotta was starting to shiver and shake. She knew what that was a sign of. She had been secretly standing in the back of the crowds that were now attending Carlotta's 'standing room only' church. She had seen Carlotta's Holy Ghost manifest and what it was capable of. She had also been told by Sandy Summer Storm how Carlotta's Holy Ghost had caused a giant crow to crap on the Reverend Pierce's head. Her own Catholic priest had slipped in holy water and sprained his back after demeaning Carlotta.

"She has to tell me what she knows about Edith White Suit." He stated not letting go of Carlotta.

"It is not Carlotta that you should be bothering about this!" Isabel sated shaking her head back and forth in a 'know it all' manner.

"I am not trying to hurt this girl. I have returned her to pastor my father's old God Assembly and to look for my red haired mother Edith. She abandoned us when I was just five or six. My mother was a Pentecostal holiness fruitcake who claimed that she was called to preach. She shamed my father by preaching in other churches. He gave up his church here because of her."

"The Edith I know is not a holiness fruit cake!" Carlotta replied in a huff, still struggling to get her arm loose. Finally, he let go of her.

Carlotta rubbed her upper arm. She was not happy about the Reverend Red Hair daring to manhandle her arm. It now ached. She rubbed it gently, while starting to pray. He may have bruised her, but she had a God and Holy Ghost that was able to heal the bruises and punish him for his assault.

Seeing that he had bruised her arm, the red haired reverend said, "I am sorry little girl about your arm. I am desperate for clues as to where my mother is. My father is dead and I have to know what happened to her. My father said she abandoned us. All I remember is her and my father quarreling about her preaching the night before she left."

"My friend Edith would not abandon a child. Furthermore, she is only about 30. She is your age and definitely too young to be your mother. Furthermore, if your mother did abandon you and your father, I am sure she was justified. You have assaulted me physically, and probably have done so because you are your father's son." Carlotta returned, rubbing her arm. "My Holy Ghost is telling me that your father probably assaulted your mother, and she fled to keep from being murdered by him. Like me, she was called to be a woman preacher, and your father wasn't called at all."

Fire lit up in the young preacher's eyes.

"I will have you know that my God Assembly father was a good man, a seminary man. He had a license to preach. It was my mother who was the uneducated idiot who listened to some illiterate independent holiness woman minister who convinced her that she was called to preach. God doesn't call women to preach. If my mother had stayed in her place in the home and at church, she would still be with us. You are just like her, a stupid little girl that doesn't know her place."

Carlotta's toe started to tingle, as she shot back asking. "God doesn't call women to preach, does he?"

"No. Women are to be submissive to their husbands, and to the male ministers of God's. Women are inferior, lower creatures in God's sight."

"I am called to preach and I can prove it!" Carlotta baited him. "Would you like to see my God and Holy Ghost come to clear up your thinking, you red haired spiritually illiterate devil in disguise?"

"You are someone's little girl who should be home helping with housework and wiping your father's shoes, instead of roam-

67

ing this town's roads." He returned in an annoyed stern voice.

"Oh . . . . Reverend Red Hair." Jose the male storekeeper interrupted, with much concern in his voice. "You don't know who this girl is. I would be careful about what you say to her."

"And just why should I be careful about what I say to her. I am just putting her in her place."

"Carlotta is the miracle working pastor of the 'Three Chairs Pentecostal Holiness Church' here in town. Carlotta is a woman minister . . . and definitely called of God."

"This ten year old kid is a minister?" the red haired reverend asked in disbelief. "You have got to be kidding."

"I am not ten. I am thirteen." Carlotta quickly interjected.

"Well you look ten to me. Who has had the gall to tell this kid that she is called to be a preacher?" He asked aiming his question to Jose.

Jose did not answer him, but proceeded to make the Catholic sign of the cross over his heart area.

"Let us put our Gods to the test. Let us both take turns praying and letting our God decide who is right on the subject of women preaching." Carlotta spit out, not backing down from the young red haired God Assembly pastor.

"She is baiting you reverend. "Isabel, the female storekeeper interrupted in a warning voice. "Don't take the bait . . . you will be sorry."

"There is nothing this girl can say or do to change my thinking. She can bait all she wants." He replied.

"Show me the power of your woman demeaning, male chauvinist God; and then I will show you the power of mine!" Carlotta shot back to him in a strong, unwavering voice.

"Alright, little girl . . . you go first! Show me your fantasy God and what he can do. I can assure you that my god and his doctrines concerning women preaching are correct. My god will most assuredly find you and your idiotic woman preacher ideas as most amusing."

"I am no idiot. What I am is called of God. I am offering you the chance once more to go first," Carlotta spit out.

"Nah . . . Go ahead you little female fantasy believing idiot, call on your god and let him crap on my head if you are right and I am wrong." He stated baiting her, fully thinking he had her and that she would be put in her place when nothing happened after she prayed.

"Oh Reverend . . . you do not know what you have said," Isabel once more interrupted stating and shaking her head at his idiocy.

"My God and Holy Ghost will show you that I am a called woman, and that you are the idiot standing in this store. I will pray precisely and ask that he send his wrath down on your head in the form of crap. Get your handkerchief out, Reverend Red Hair, you are going to need it."

"What a ridiculous idea to pray for." He instantly returned, shaking his head in disgust. "You are wasting your time."

Carlotta felt the power of the Holy Ghost start to move up her leg, her body, and then her right arm which she threw up into the air. She then began to speak in tongues.

Jo Hammers

"Run Reverend . . . Run!" Isabel the storekeeper shouted. "She is about to call for crow crap to fall on you. She will call it down and it will land right on your wavy, red hair, just like it did on Reverend Pierce's. "

"I am not running from this misled little girl who is full of fantasy beliefs and definitely misguided." He stated, folding his arms across his chest and giving Carlotta a dare you stare.

For a brief moment, Carlotta returned to speaking in human language and said, "I am God called . . . not misguided."

"You are a little girl lost in her fantasies." He returned staring harder at her. "A woman's place is in the home, not behind a sacred pulpit."

Carlotta did not back up or give in an inch.

"So, you think a woman's place is only as a door mat for little men like you who want to be big men, but don't you know how?"

"I am not a little man, and 'Yes' I believe that I, as a man, am head of any woman at home, out in public, or in the church. Women are inferior creatures and are to be submissive to their husbands and male ministers."

Carlotta's big toe started to tingle again. She threw her right hand into the air and began to pray, "Holy Ghost come now! Avenge me and all women like me that are called of God to preach. Show this man that he is the one that is wrong in his thinking concerning women. Let your wrath fall now on his head as a sign. Let many forms of wrath fall on his head, like the plagues fell on Egypt and its Pharaoh in the Old Testament, when he wouldn't let Moses' people go."

With her prayer sent up in words that the young red haired

preacher could understand, Carlotta then began to speak in un-known tongues and then started to shiver, shake, and dance in the Holy Ghost.

The surprised young preacher backed up a little, not quite sure what his sudden strange encounter with the dancing, mis-led, little thirteen year old girl was all about. Then it happened, a huge Tom cat appeared out of nowhere and started walking along the over head beam above them, where baskets of this and that hung from hooks in the beam. The cat crept along the nar-row wooden over head beam till it reached a position directly over the young preacher's head. For some reason, the male cat spotted the red hair of the young minister, and decided to mark his territory. In an instant, a spray of stinking cat urine fell on the head of the God Assembly minister. In shock, the young preacher immediately tried to wipe the urine from his eyes with his hands. However, the cat wasn't thru. It seemed to suddenly be sick and instantly vomited up all the contents of its stomach, an eaten rat, and it came puking down on the top of the urine covered red haired preacher. The young minister wiped furi-ously to get the half eaten rat pieces off of his face. However, the cat still wasn't thru. Instantly, the cat turned and let his bowels explode expelling watery diarrhea. It fell like rain on top of the vomit and the urine.

Isabel and Jose stood with their mouths open in shock. They had heard about the wrath miracles that followed Carlotta, but this was their first up front moment of seeing one. Both of the Catholic market owners in unison made the sign of the cross again.

The young red haired minister continued to struggle to wipe the stench mess from his eyes, nose and mouth.

A miracle of wrath happened avenging Carlotta. However another miracle occurred. Not a single drop of the urine, vomit, or cat crap had landed on Carlotta, Isabel, Jose, or the market's floor.

Finally getting his eyes cleared, he glanced at Isabel.

"I told you to run!" Isabel scolded the young minister in a raised annoyed voice.

When the Holy Ghost power lifted, Carlotta opened her eyes and she laughingly stated as the red haired man spit a piece of rat vomit from his mouth, "My God and Holy Ghost have shown up to avenge me! Where is your god?"

The red haired young minister could not answer her. He was too busy trying to get the mess off of his face and nose so that he could breathe properly.

Carlotta, laughing, turned and started to walk out the front screen door of the little 'mom and pop' market. Suddenly, she turned and looked back at the young reverend and directly into his eyes. She only thought God and the Holy Ghost was thru with her.

Suddenly, the voice of God spoke thru Carlotta and it was a powerful voice of divine authority. "Touch not my anointed, and do my prophetess no harm. I know Edith White Suit. I know Carlotta. I know your mother. Who are you?"

Shocked by the voice of God, the cat vomit and diarrhea covered, red haired reverend ran from the market, got in his pickup and sped away as though he were frightened out of his gourd.

Isabel turned to her husband Jose as Carlotta exited. "I tried to warn him. No one ever listens to me."

Jose, the male market owner, just smiled. He was now dead

serious in his thinking about leaving the Catholic Church and becoming one of the Pentecostal, Holy Ghost filled, called ones. He had been having dreams of being filled with the Holy Ghost to overflowing. He wanted a god that actually spoke to him, like Carlotta's did. He had gone to regular confession in the Catholic Church his whole life, but God had never spoken to him there. The only voice he had ever heard was that of the priest telling him how many 'Hail Mary's' to say.

Jose feared asking Carlotta to become a member of her church. She did not seem to have much respect for men. He had decided he would have to earn her respect before asking. In the back of his mind he could see himself pulling up all of Rosa Garcia's flowers and secretly pouring a new cement floor the size of the flower garden. He had decided he would pour the cement large enough for the three chairs, a speaking area up front, and room enough behind the chairs for at least fifty people to stand. Carlotta's church was a standing up room only church. He decided he would have the cement poured by a construction crew one day when Carlotta went back to school. He had already secretly approached Carlotta's father, Hidalgo, about it. Her father had agreed to the project, but added that they might have to run if Rosa's feet got suddenly well and she started chasing them with her broom. Otherwise, they would just listen to her yell and go ahead with a cement church floor for Carlotta.

After pouring the secret cement floor, it was Jose's intention to go forward in service and ask to be filled with Carlotta's Holy Ghost and to become a member of her 'standing room only' church.

CHAPTER ELEVEN

Without Honor

School had been in session for about three weeks when Carlotta's father pulled her from her classes because her mother Rosa had been taken by ambulance to the hospital. Rosa's two sprained ankles had never healed and one toe on each of her feet had suddenly started turning black over night. The doctor had already seen Rosa before Hidalgo and Carlotta got to the hospital. His news to her was not good.

Carlotta pulled back a white curtain and entered a little curtain closed off cubicle where her mother lay crying in a hospital bed. Her father Hidalgo entered behind her.

"Why are you crying, mama?" Carlotta asked walking up to the hospital rails up bed and leaning over to kiss her mother on the forehead. Carlotta then took her mother's hand and held it in hers.

"I am going to die, Carlotta. I am diabetic and my two feet are developing gangrene from the sprains. My toes are turning black because my feet are dying. The doctor says my two feet must come off. He says if I don't agree to it, I will die within a short time."

Hidalgo, teary eyed, took his wife Rosa's other hand in his. "Now Rosa, lots of people live with amputated limbs."

"It is not losing limbs that I am worried about, Hidalgo. It is Carlotta. If I do not have well feet to chase her with my broom from my flower garden, she will always be possessed of that Holy Ghost devil that makes her dance and preach protestant ideas. Without feet, I cannot get all those people out of my flower bed and Carlotta to the Catholic Church for her exorcism. Without me, she is lost to the gringo, devil possessed Protestants."

Carlotta let go of her mother's hand. Then, with the greatest of sadness and tears falling from her eyes, Carlotta realized that her mother would never see her, or accept her for the called woman of God she was. With tears streaming down her face, Carlotta headed for the waiting area to find a quiet place in a corner somewhere to deal with her hurt feelings and sorrow. When reaching there she spotted Edith White Suit standing outside the emergency room's pair of sliding doors.

Quickly walking past a couple of rolling gurneys with incoming patients, Carlotta made her way to Edith who was standing barefoot next to one of the ambulances that had just unloaded.

"Edith . . ." Carlotta called in a raised voice to get the barefoot woman's attention before she walked away. Then Carlotta ran into her arms.

"What is wrong, Carlotta?" Edith White Suit asked while holding and comforting the thirteen year old girl.

After a moment or so, Carlotta regained her composure and backed off from Edith so that she could talk to her.

"My mother, Rosa, has been told by the doctor that she must have her two feet taken off, or she will die. I know my God can heal her, Edith. However, she will not let me pray for her. Instead, as she lies in her hospital cubicle inside, she is ranting on and on about her needing to get a Catholic exorcism for me. She is telling everyone in her cubicle that my Holy Ghost is a devil that has possessed me."

"I am so sorry, Carlotta."

"My mother is going to die, Edith White Suit, never seeing that I am called of God or that my Holy Ghost filled Pentecostal experience is real. She is going to die thinking that I am possessed by an evil spirit."

"There are some sorrows we must endure when we are called of God, Carlotta. The bible says a prophet is without honor in his own country. All your family and friends will not necessarily accept the fact that God has chosen you (a woman) to be his anointed one."

"I love my mother, Edith White Suit. Her denial of me and my calling sorrows me to the core of my being." Carlotta spit out in despair.

"There are many women in God's service besides you that are sorrowed to the core of their being, just like you. Their family and friends have turned their backs on them, just as your mother has now done to you."

"My friend Wendy, at school, has quit being friends with me. She now calls me a Holy Ghost freak. Her words hurt me, just like the words of my mother."

"When you are my age, Carlotta, you will look back and possibly not even remember Wendy. I am not friends today with those I attended Kindergarten and elementary school with, so many . . . many years ago. I have grown up and no longer need kindergarten friends to play 'tea party' and 'dolls' with. With each phase of my life from elementary school to college and beyond I have made new friends in each school experience. You will make new friends with every new phase of your calling to preach happens. Wendy is now your past "tea party' and 'dolls' friend. She cannot understand or go with you on your new journey into the ministry. She sleeps spiritually and therefore has no understanding of your calling, the Holy Ghost, etc. She sleeps spiritually and so does your Mother, Rosa."

"I will have new friends?" Carlotta asked thru tears.

"Yes, Carlotta, you must let go of your old friend to let a new one come into your life." Edith replied in a gentle voice. "We must let go to receive. We must let everything in our lives flow out so that a new flow can come in."

"Will my mother flow away from me in death?" Carlotta asked, fully knowing what the answer was.

"Man has free will choice, Carlotta. It is a gift from God that God does not interfere with. Your mother has free will choice. She must choose whether to support you or not support you in your calling to preach. If she does not, God will take her. He will not let her stand in your way and the building of your church on her flower garden spot. You are the anointed and called one. She is not. She sleeps spiritually."

"I understand what you are saying to me, Edith White Suit. However, I am deeply sorrowed about the thought of my mother dying."

"Sorrow comes, but sorrow will flow out. Behind every sorrow storm in life, is sunshine on the way to you."

"Thank you, Edith White Suit. I needed your words of wisdom. I will continue my walk forward in God, even though my family and friends flow away from me."

"Go with God! Carlotta." Edith returned.

"I must return inside now to be support for my father Hidalgo and brother, Pablo. Did you know that they are both attending my 'Three Chair Church' regularly?" Carlotta asked with a bit of sunshine returning to her face.

Edith smiled warmly and then gave Carlotta a parting hug.

Walking back into the hospital thru the emergency room doors, Carlotta turned briefly just inside the glass doors to wave goodbye to Edith. Barefoot Edith White Suit, dressed in holiness white, was not there and would never be seen again.

Rosa Garcia did die, insisting to the end that her daughter was devil possessed.

After his wife's death, Hidalgo Garcia supported his daughter in her calling and attended her services regularly.

Pablo Garcia eventually answered his own call to enter the Pentecostal ministry. He moved to Dallas and started a three chair church in the back of a motor cycle repair shop he opened.

Isabel and Jose, the Hispanic 'mom and pop' market owners, became members of Carlotta's church. After Rosa's death, Jose did pour a concrete church floor for Carlotta.

The red haired young minister lasted only three months as pastor of the God Assembly down the road. All but three of his members, abandoned him and his church in favor of attending Carlotta's open air church. He found no clues as to the whereabouts of his mother.

Father Juan's pains from his back injury became worse and worse till he ended up in a nursing home where he couldn't move from the neck down. After three years flat of his back, he admitted to himself that his words demeaning Carlotta's calling were the reason for his misery. He sent for Carlotta and asked her to forgive him for his denial of her calling. She prayed for him and he sat up and got out of bed. He was healed of the back injury that had paralyzed him. Father Juan left the Catholic Church and became a lay member in Carlotta's 'Three Chairs Church'.

Sister Margaret answered her call to preach in one of Carlotta's 'standing room only' meetings. She became a healing evangelist, and spoke and prayed for the sick in churches all over the southwest.

Wendy, Carlotta's school friend became a ballet teacher as an adult, and remained Baptist and a thorn in Carlotta's side the rest of her life. Wendy wrote letters to Carlotta often over the years telling her that she was dying and going to hell for not being submissive and letting a man be the head of her and her three chair church. In her forties, Wendy died at the hands of her control freak Baptist husband. Her deacon husband beat her to death, in spite of her loyalty and letting him be the head of her household.

Carlotta never married. Her allegiance was to God. Every summer, till the day she crossed over, she would erect a big white tent over her mother's flower garden patch and hold a tent meeting, so that other girls and women like her could be called. Jose's poured piece of cement would become the platform podium area for the summer tent revivals. She always had standing room only crowds. If anyone wanted a chair to sit in, they had to bring it with them to church.

Jo Hammers

After the hospital episode with Rosa dying, Edith White Suit was never seen again. Native American, Sandy Summer Storm, insisted till her death that Edith in the White suit was her White Buffalo Woman, just like Carlotta's God was her Great White Spirit.

CHAPTER TWELVE

The Call to Preach

I f you are a woman reading this book, God is calling you to work for him. This is your trumpet sound.

If you are called to build a church for God, all you need is three chairs and a place to stand in front of them to speak. The three chairs can be your kitchen chairs or a park bench. Where two or three are gathered together in God's name, God will come down and be in the midst. You do not need a building, hymnals, wooden altar, piano, or any other manmade object to start a church. All you need is three chairs and a willingness to preach in whatever flower garden patch he plants you and your chairs in. God will show you where to place your three chairs.

Your flower garden patch could be in a student lounge, a park, the top of your apartment building or its laundry room. Your flower garden patch could be in your living room, a parking lot, or the lounge of a truck stop. Pray and ask God where you are to place your three chairs.

My mission (or calling as a writer) is to help ten women start new Pentecostal, Holy Ghost filled, powerhouse churches. If ten women read this book and answer their call to become three chair church pastors, I have fulfilled my mission.

I am the trumpet sound, your trumpet sound. Answer your call!

THE END

www.ingramcontent.com/pod-product-compliance
Lightning Source LLC
Chambersburg PA
CBHW071455070426
42452CB00040B/1532